Wendy Martin

Enchanted Fantasy Art Nouveau

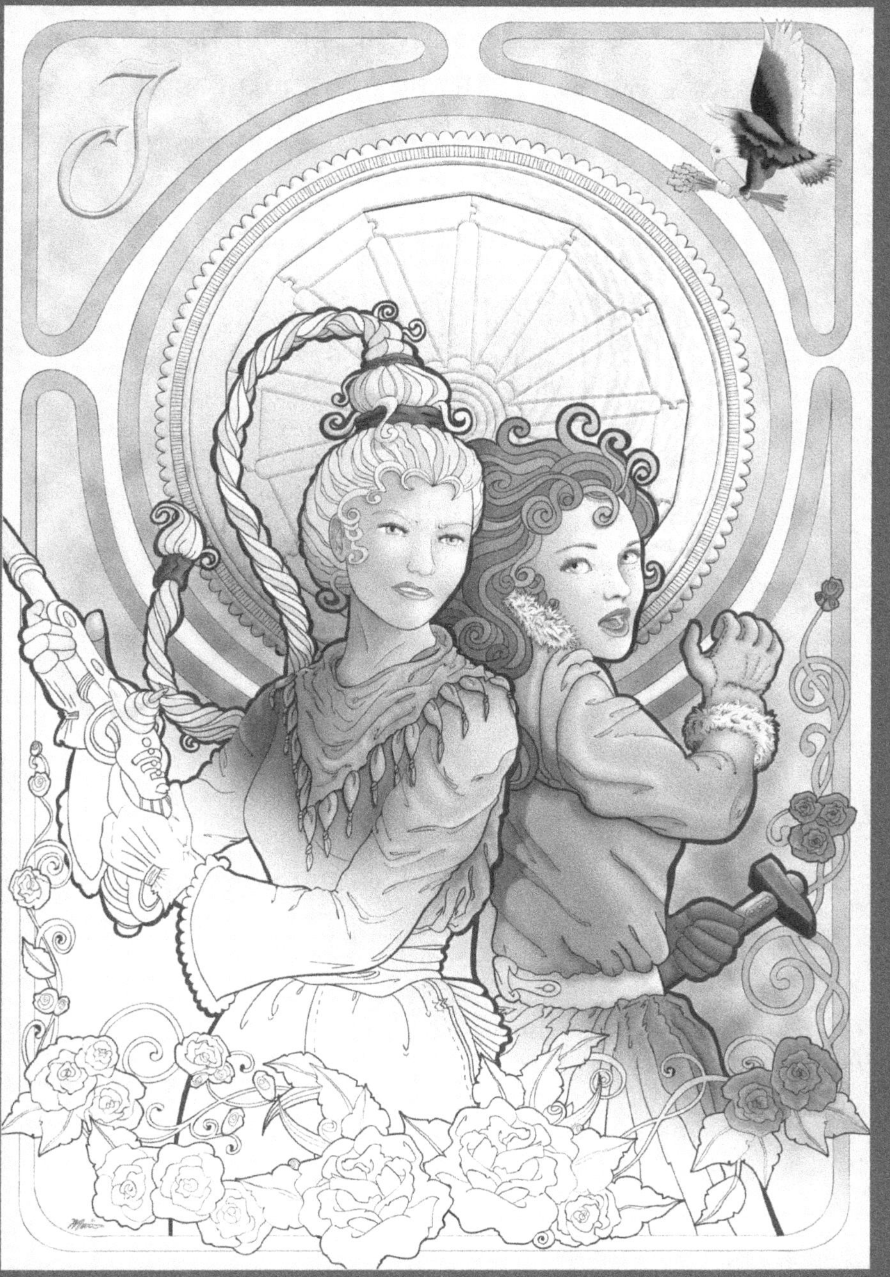

an Art Nouveau coloring book for big kids

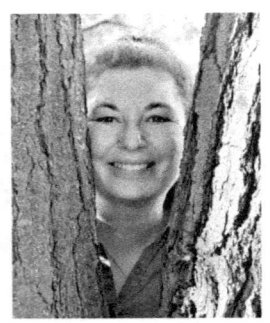

A transplanted New Yorker now living in Missouri, **Wendy Martin** has been working as an illustrator for 25+ years. Wendy's love affair with art began at an early age. One of her earliest memories is of sitting with a pile of crayons and papers strewn around her proclaiming to her parents that someday everyone in the world would be looking at her art. Her career began in advertising and graphic design in New York, in 2000, she turned her focus to her true love, children's books. *An Ordinary Girl, A Magical Child*, released in 2008, became a finalist in the 2009 international COVR awards. She most recently illustrated *The Story Circle*, released May 2016. Wendy traded in her crayons for watercolor, pen and ink, and a computer.

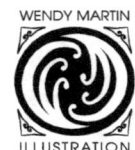

WENDY MARTIN

ILLUSTRATION

www.wendymartinillustration.com

Enchanted Fantasy Art Nouveau: an Art Nouveau coloring book for big kids

The illustrations created digitally in Adobe™ Illustrator.

ISBN 978-1523716227

Summary: A book of 21 Art Nouveau fantasy themed coloring pages.

Printed in the U.S.A.

(Original art showcased in this book was created between the years of 2010 - 2015. To see the full color images, please visit the web site above.)

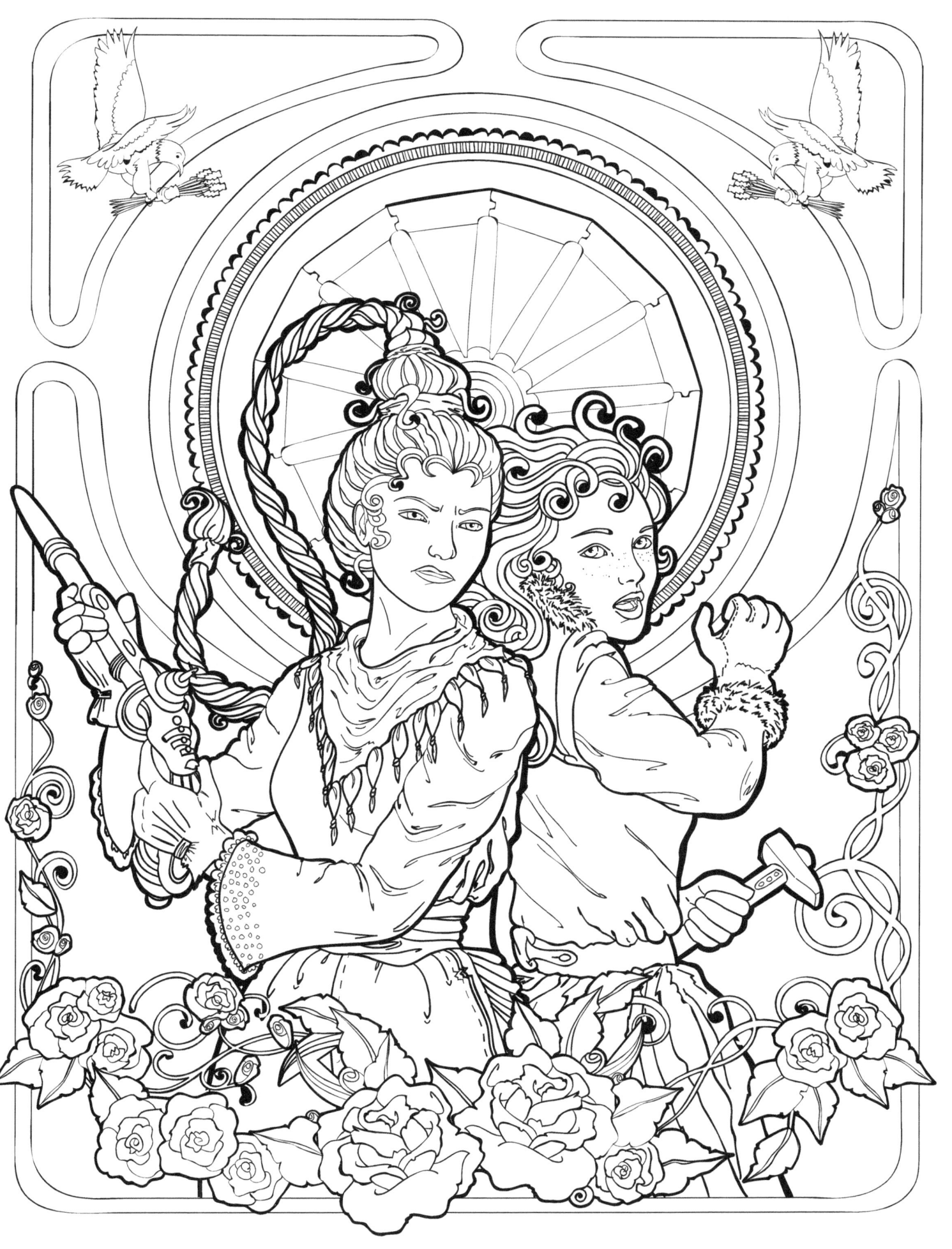

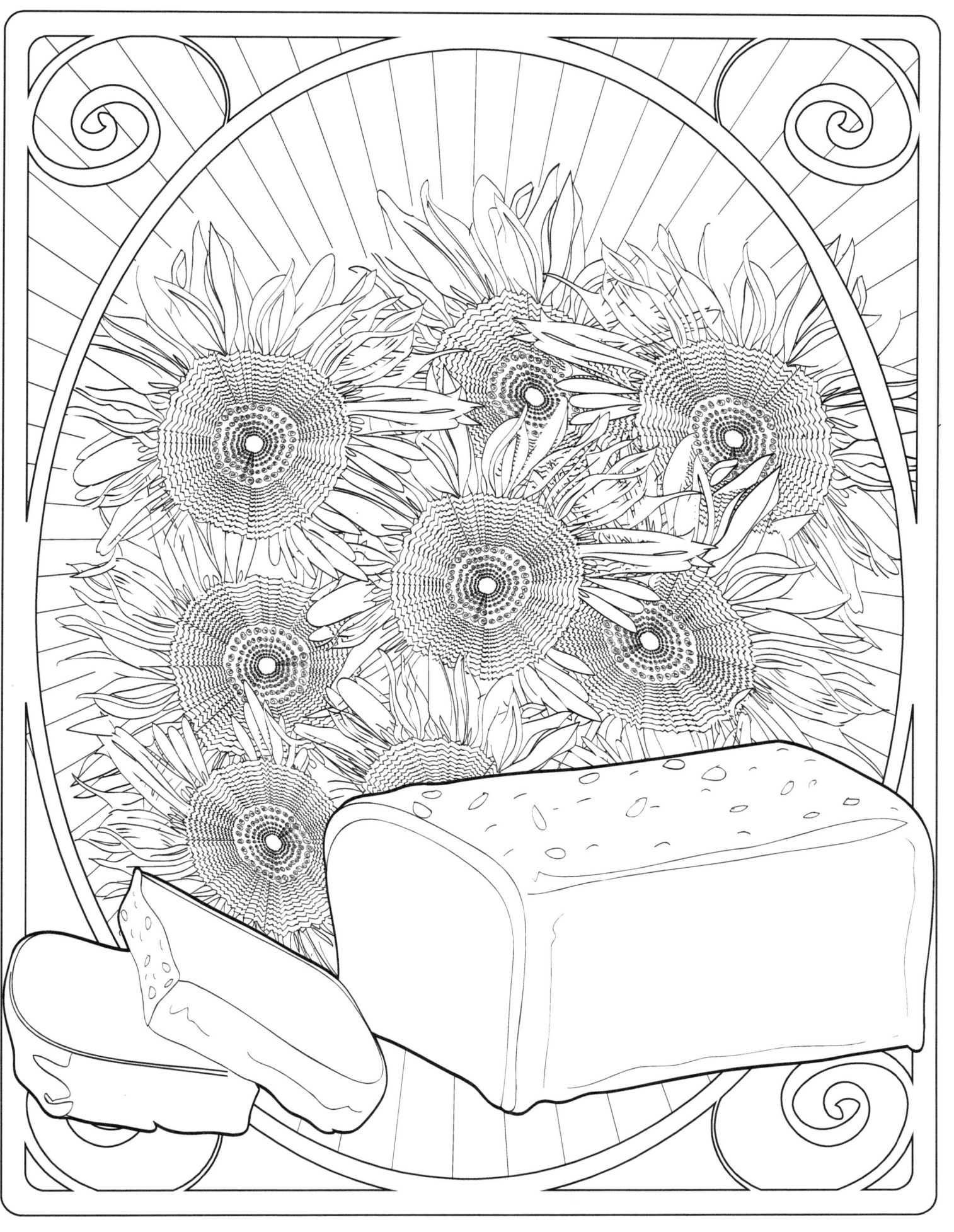

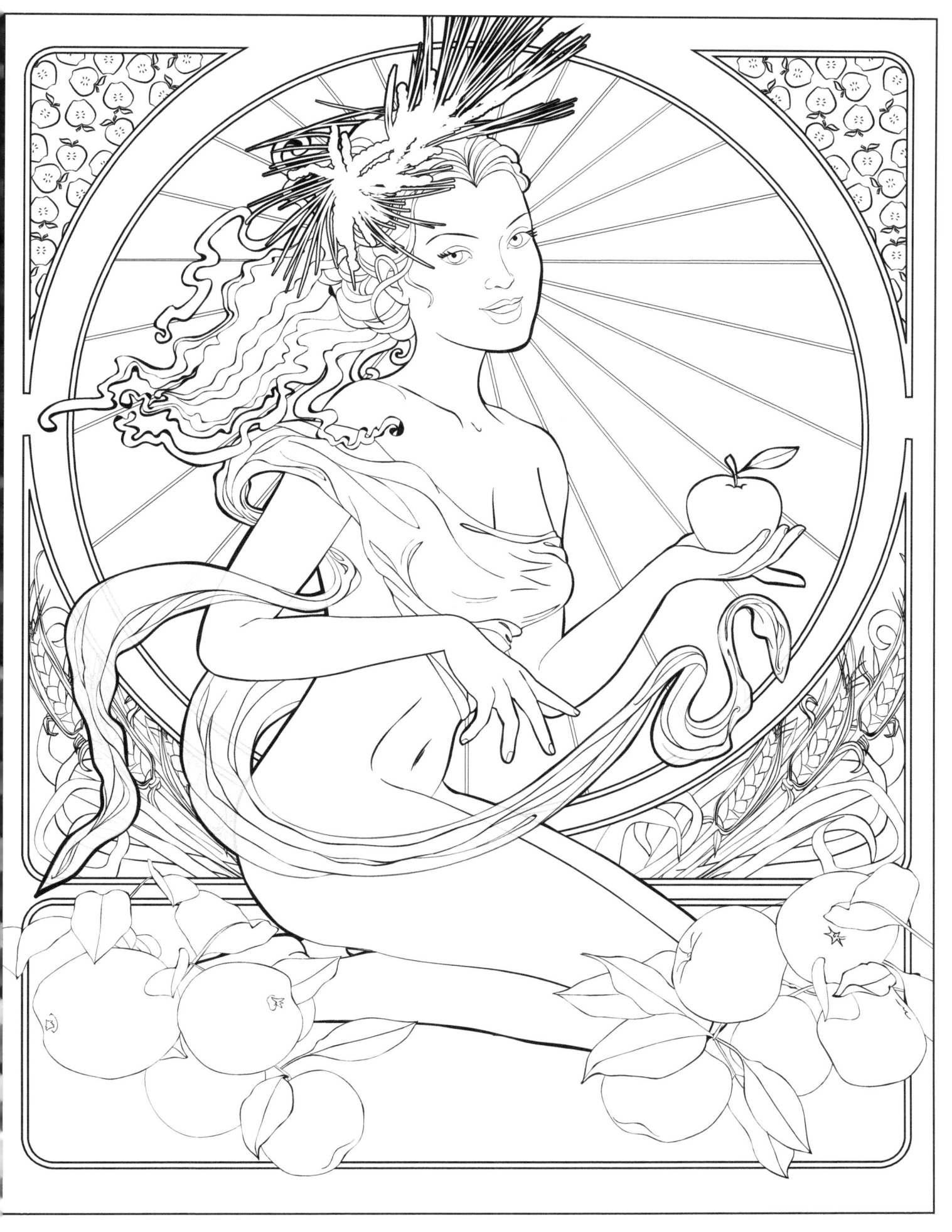

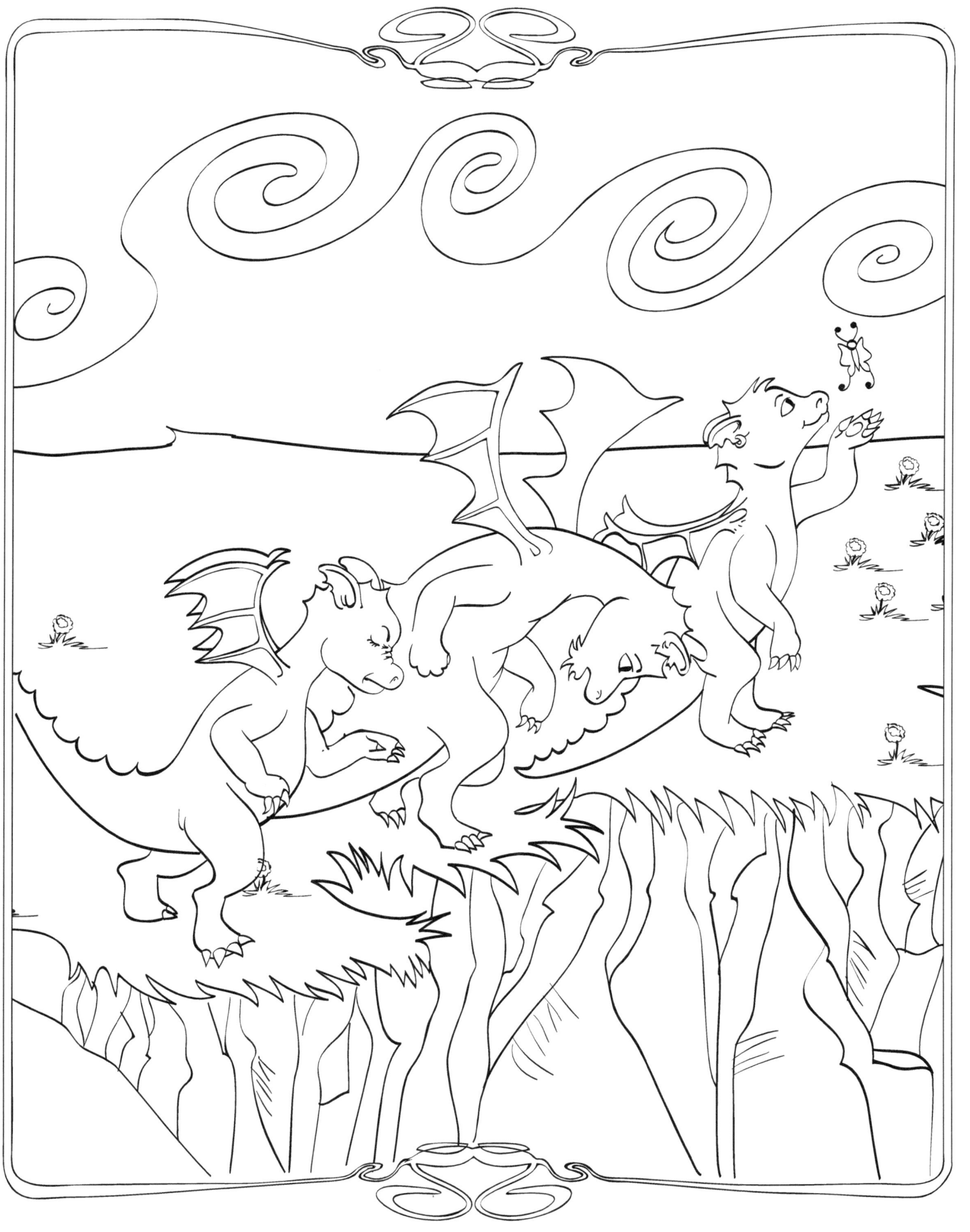

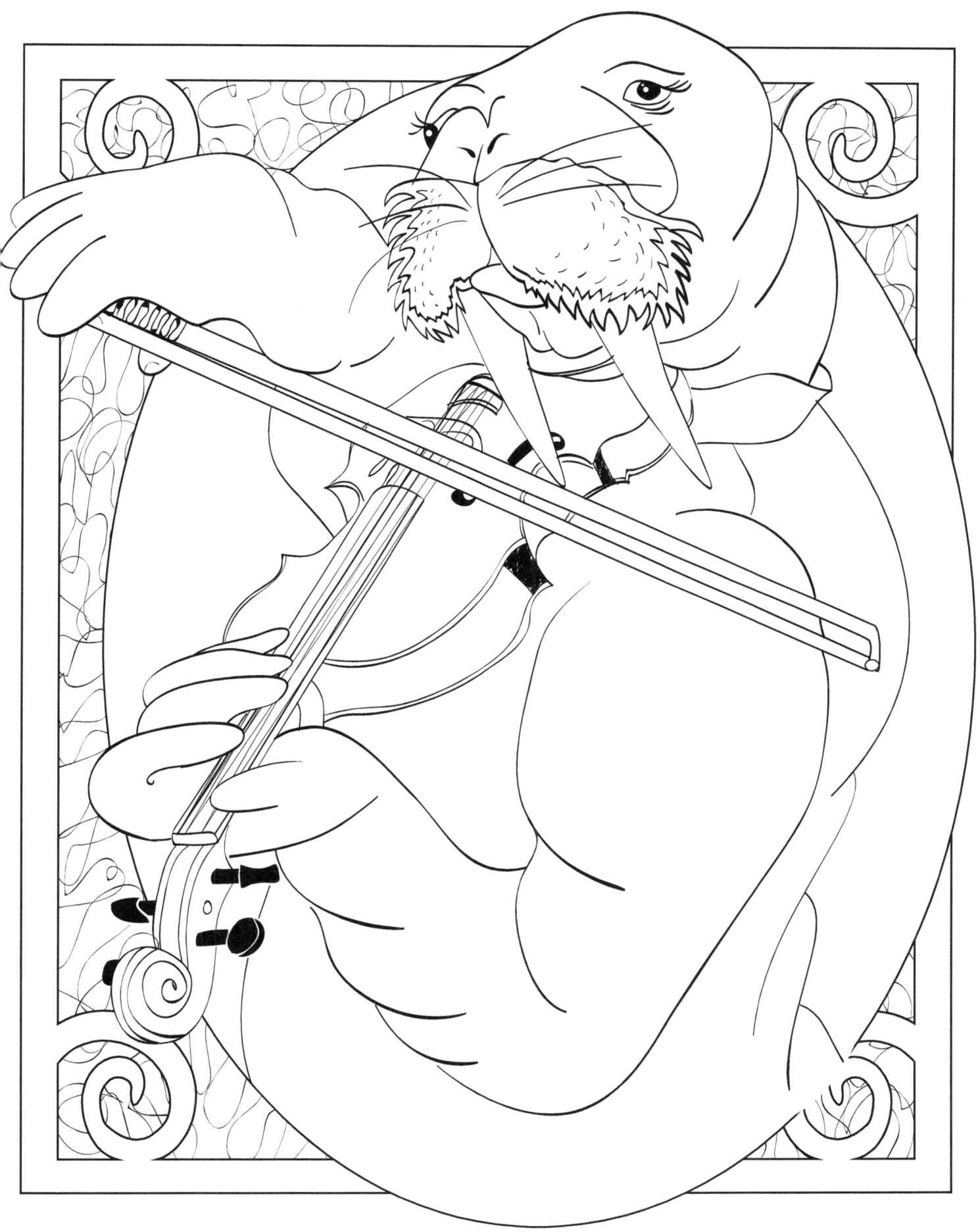

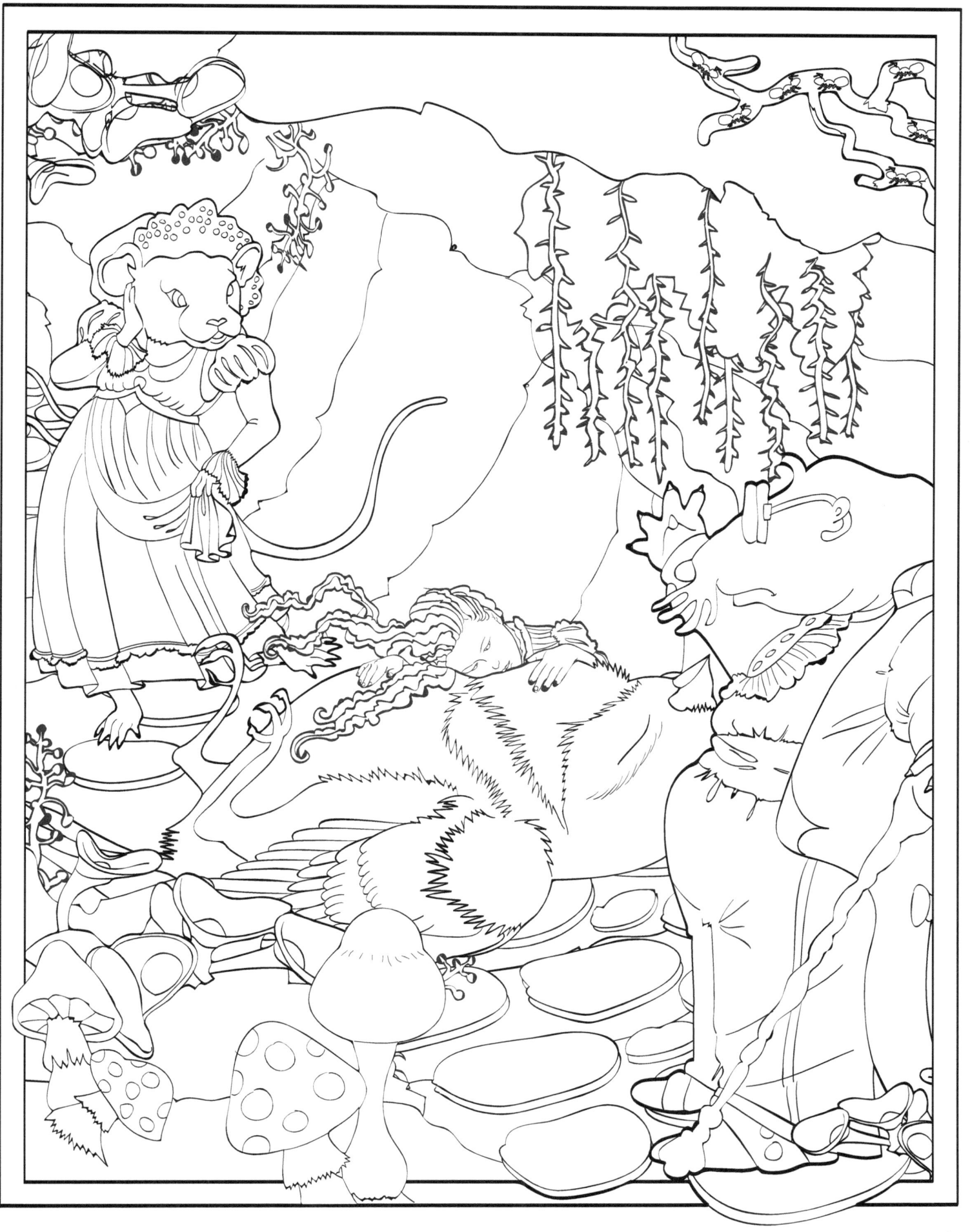

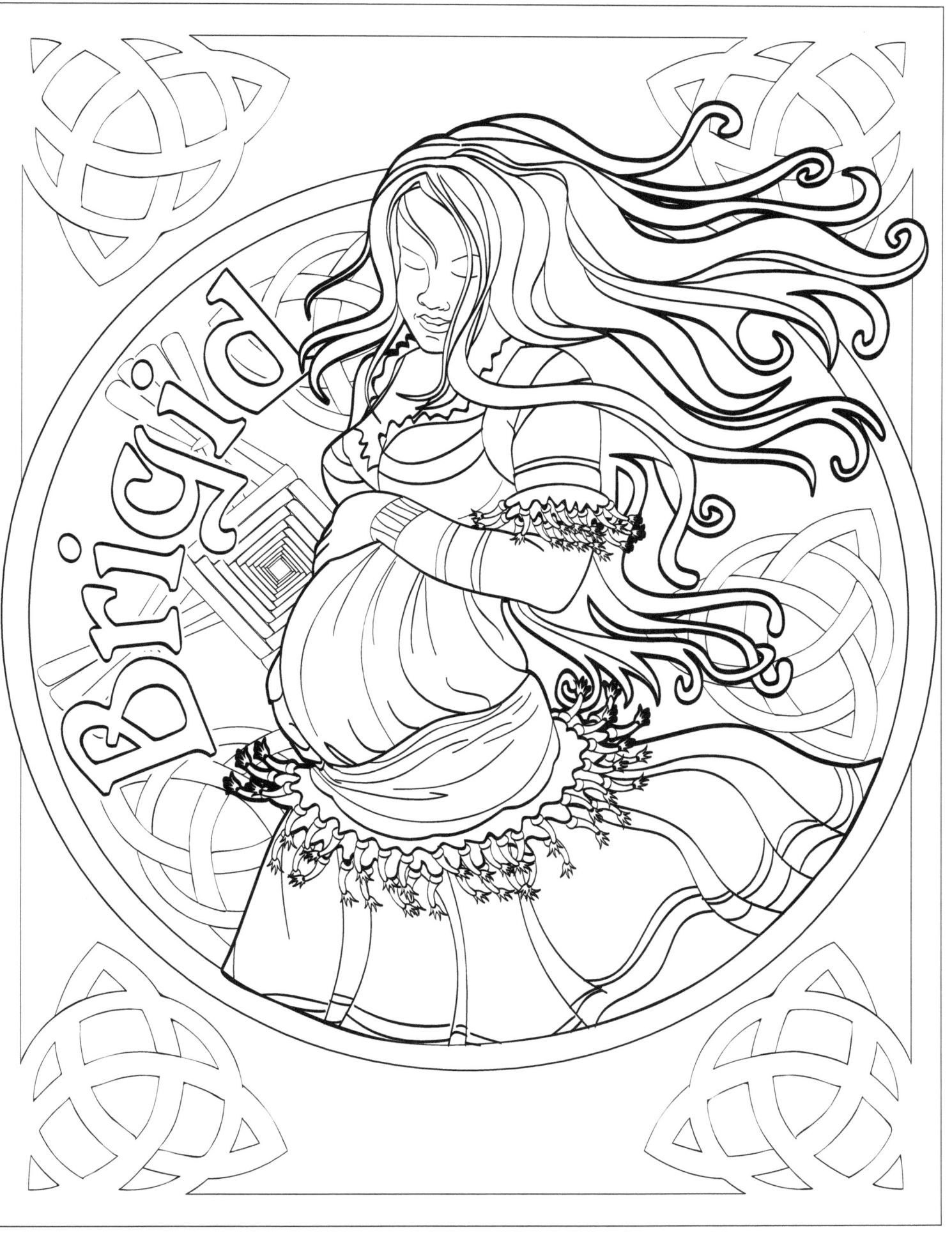

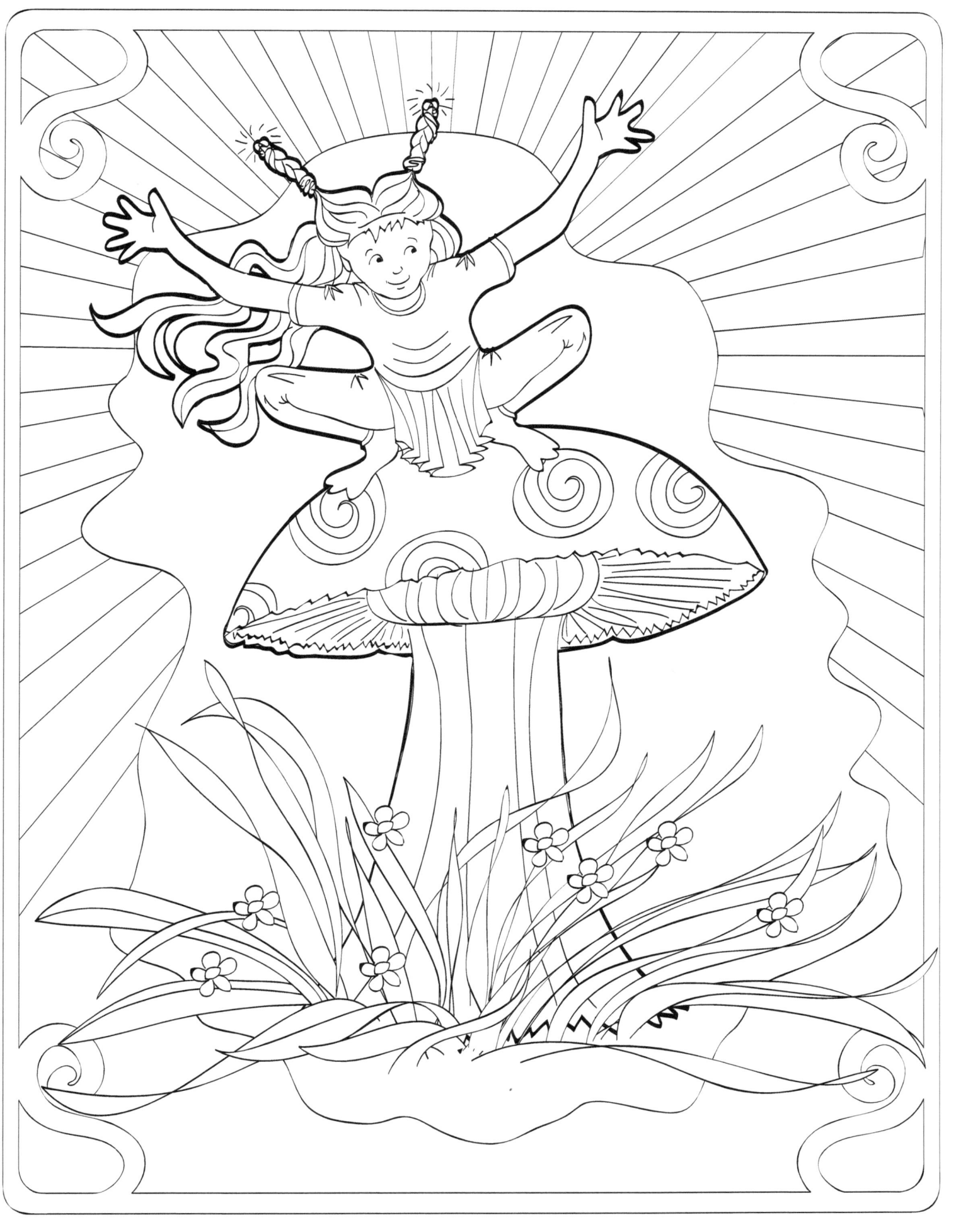

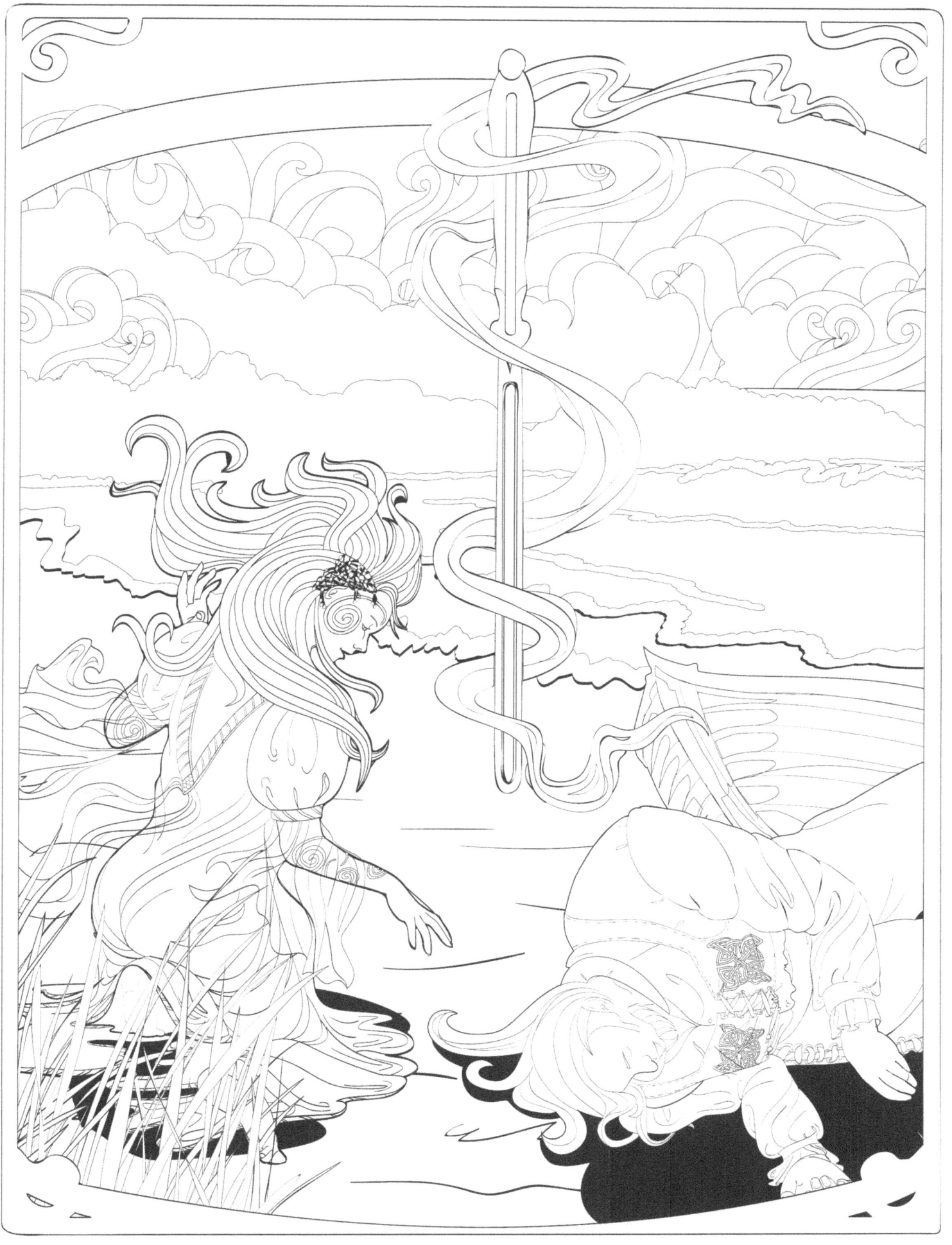

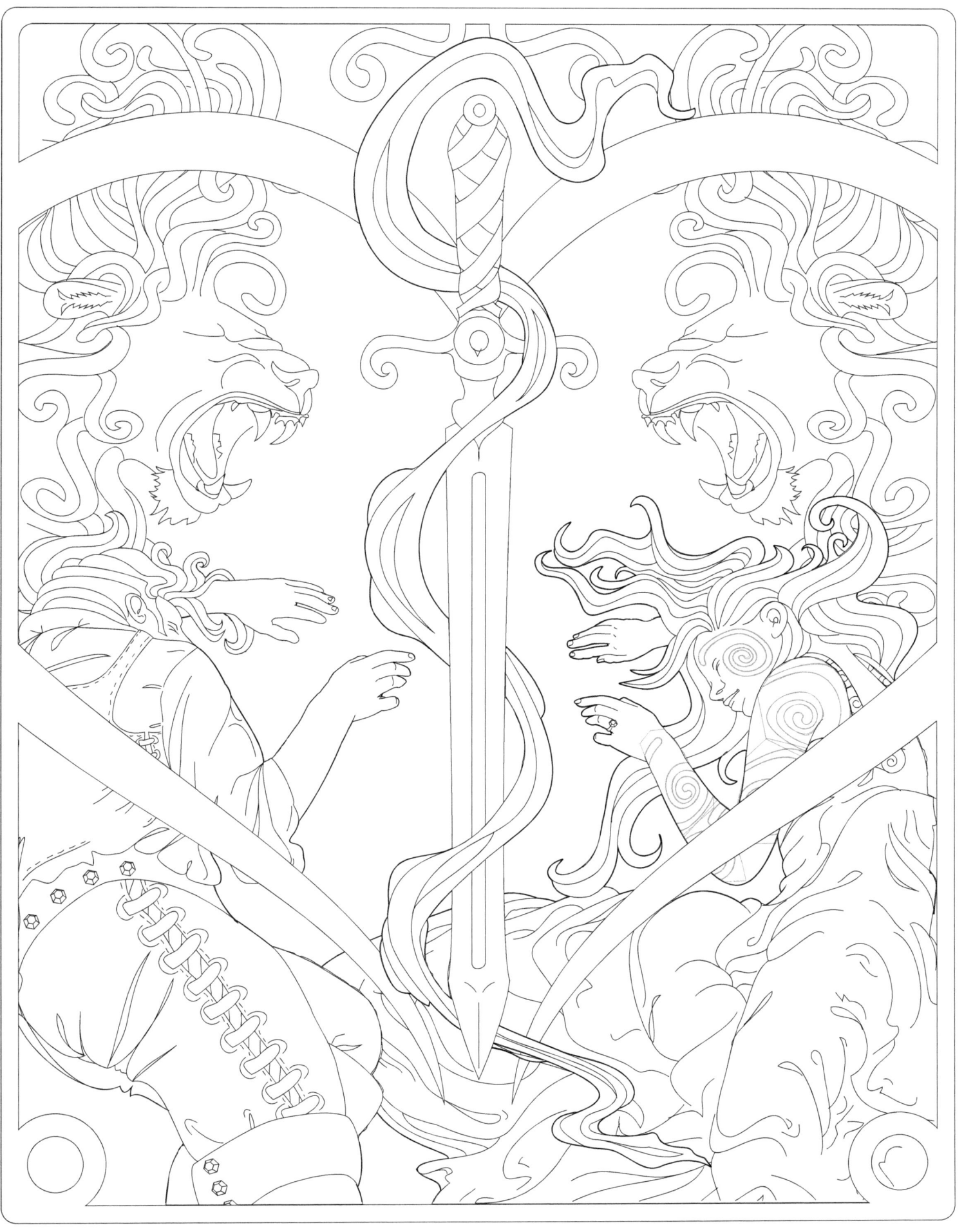

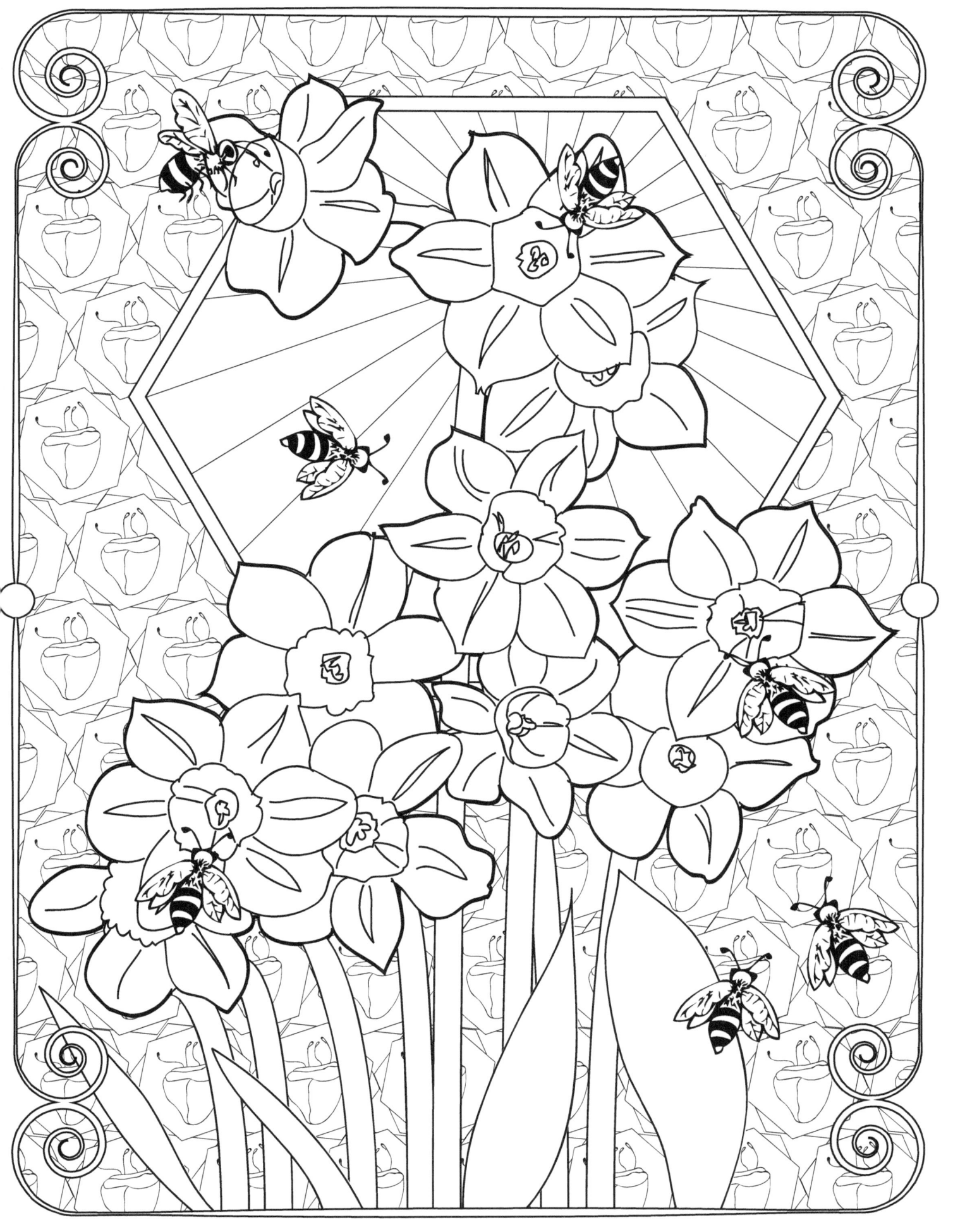

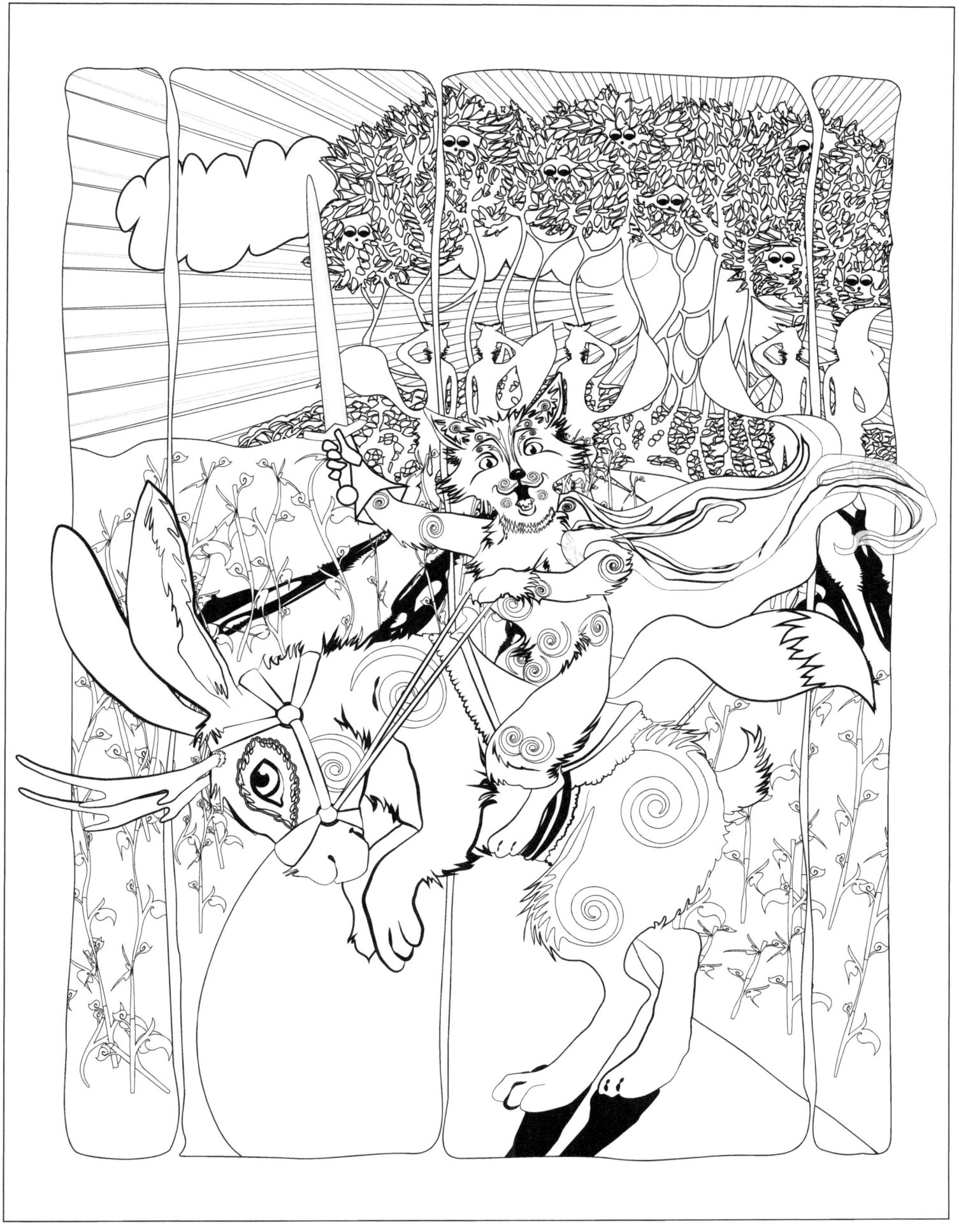

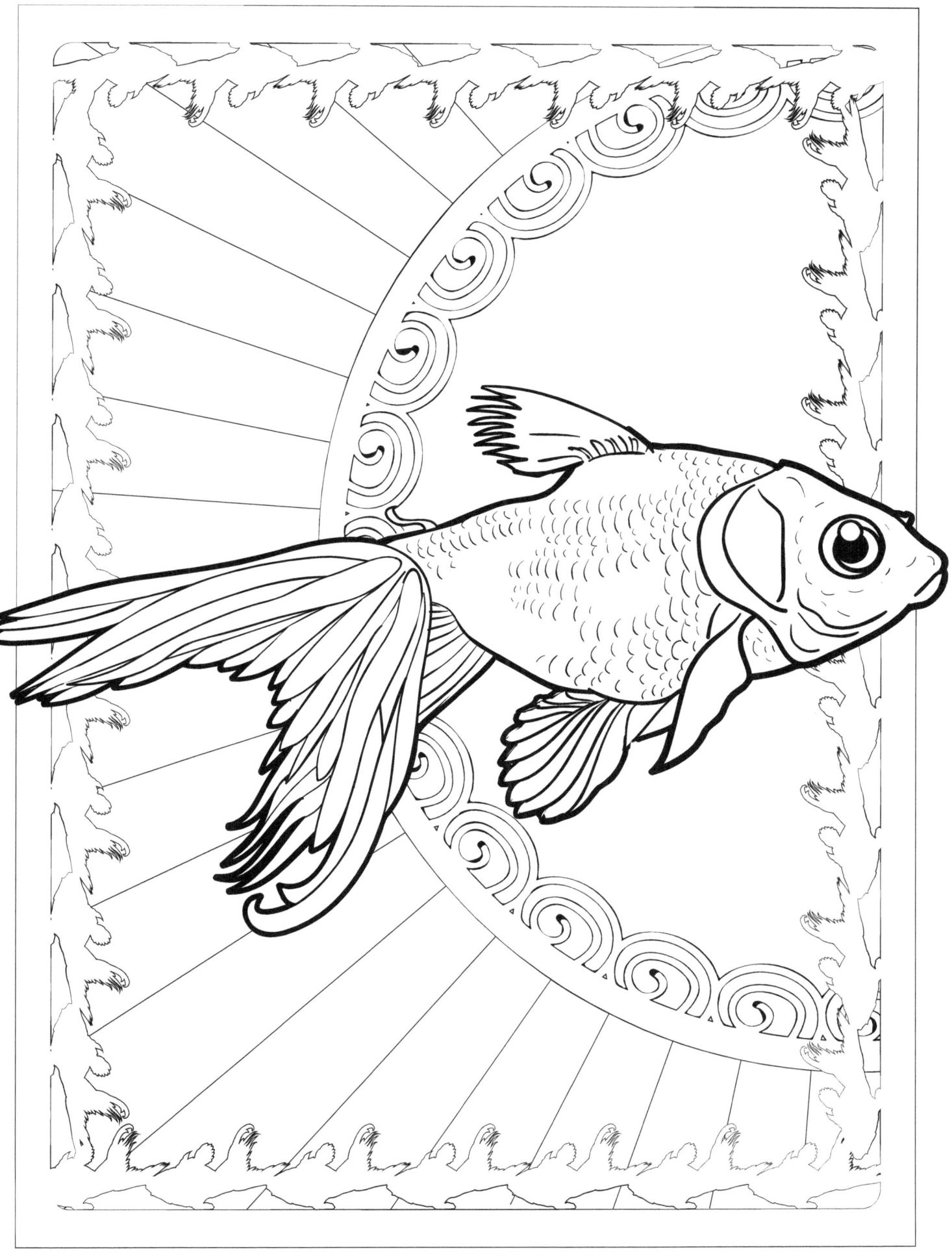

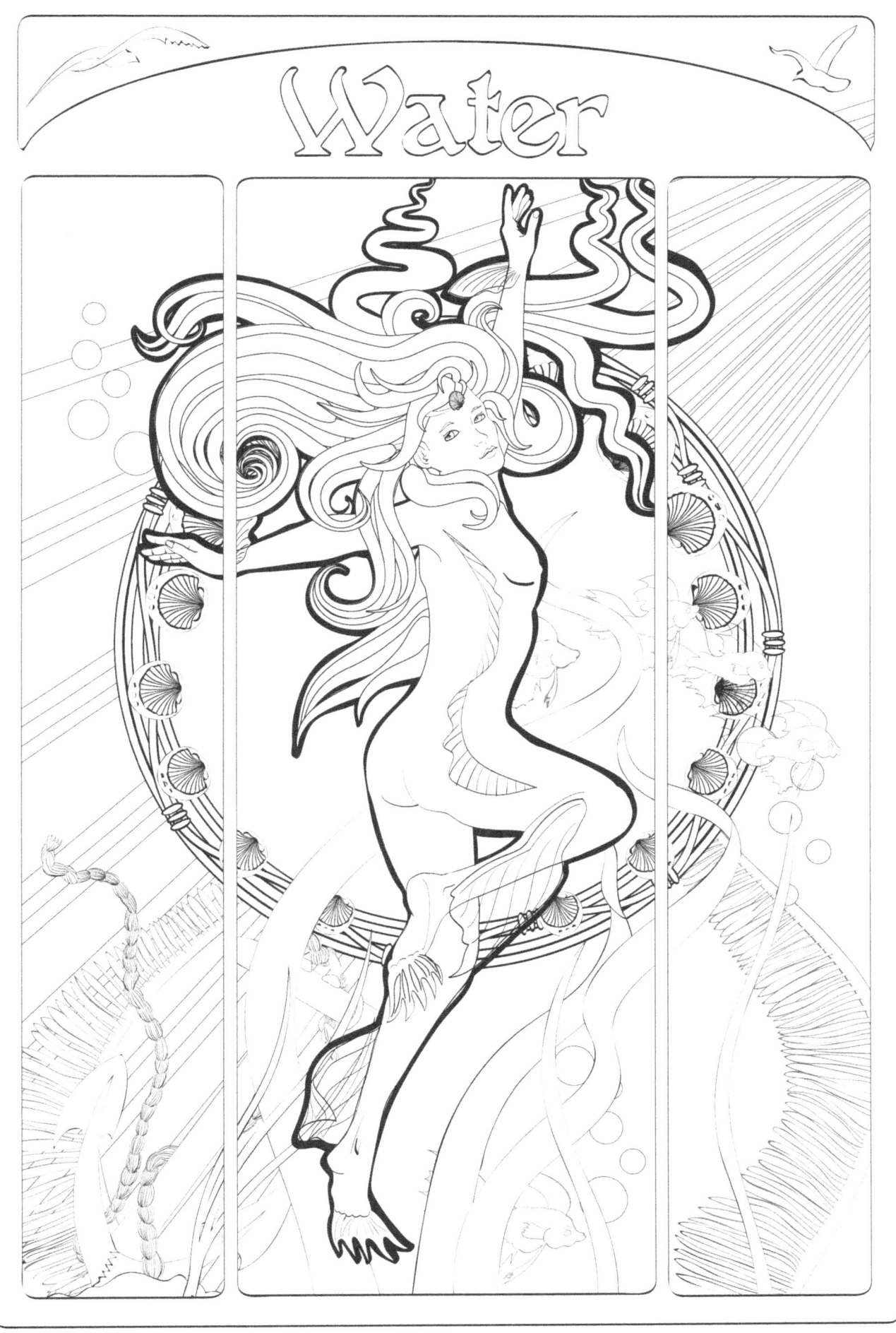

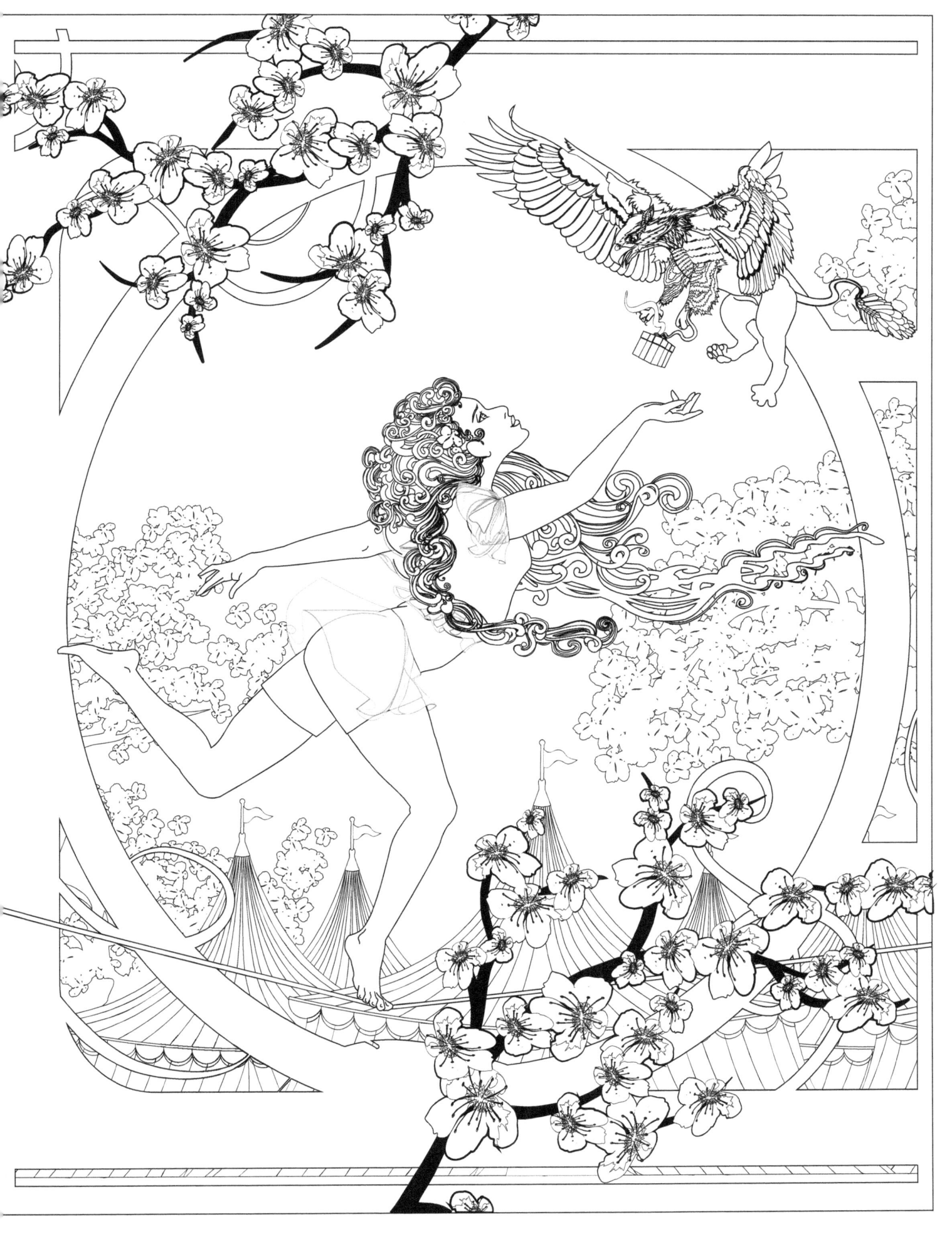

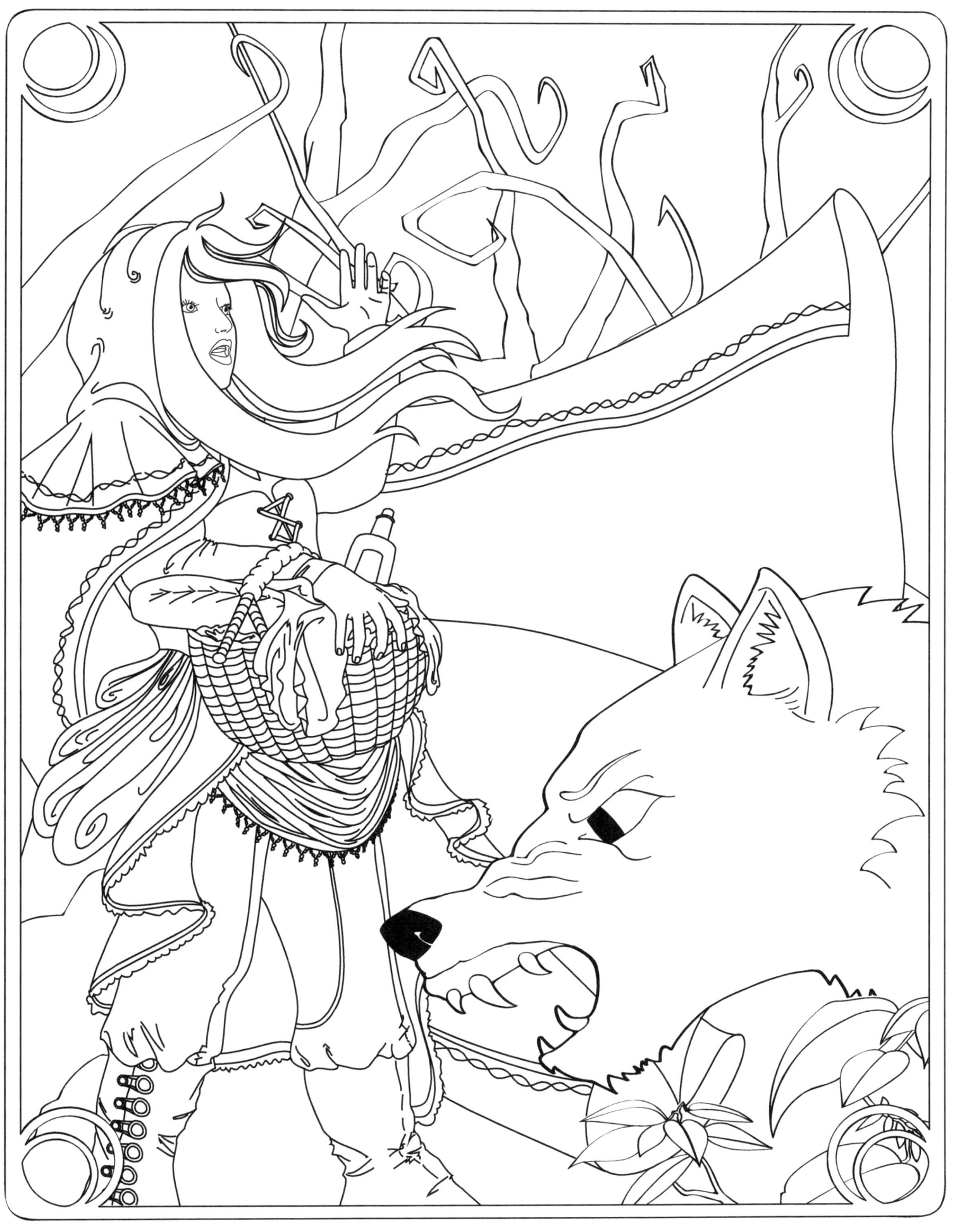

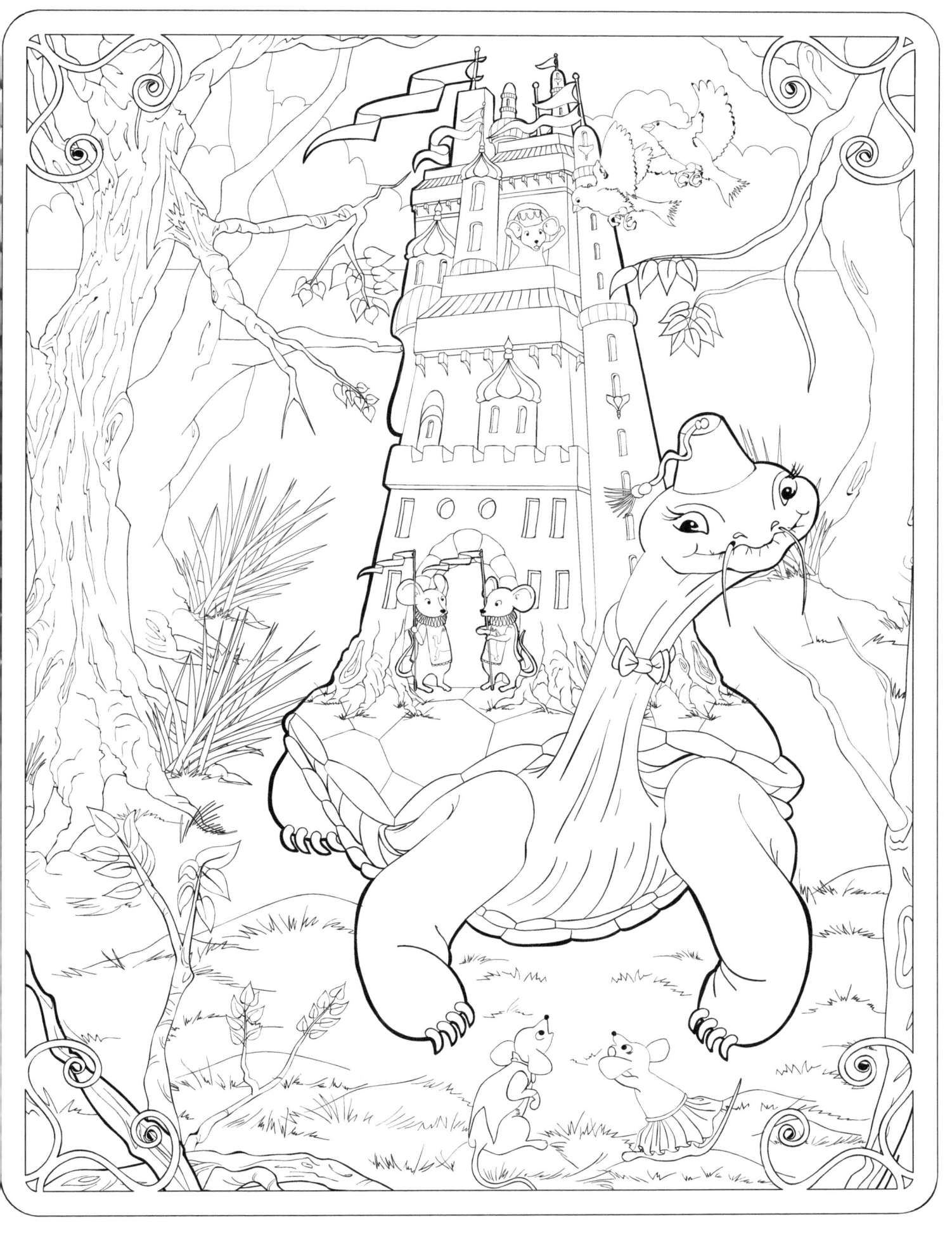

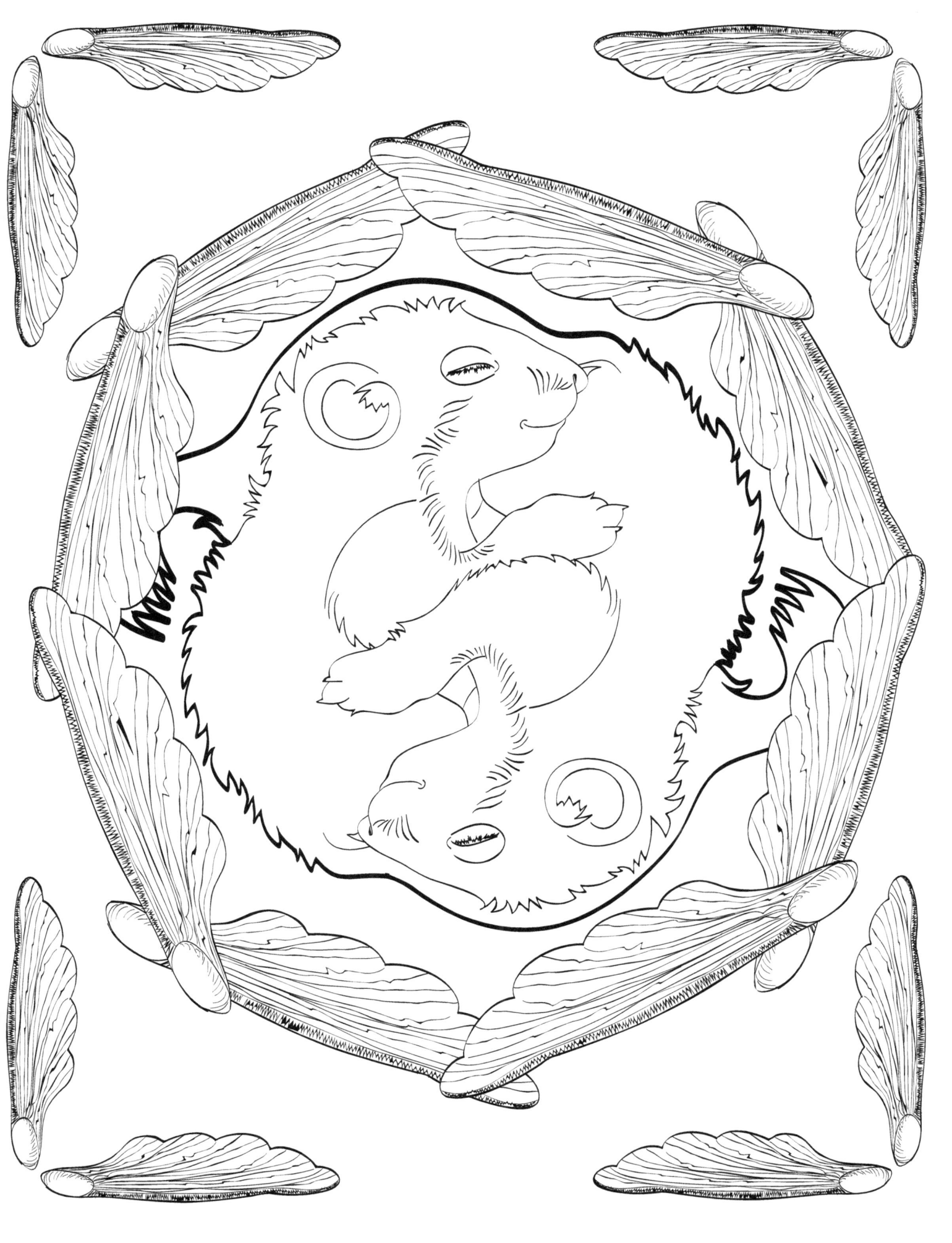

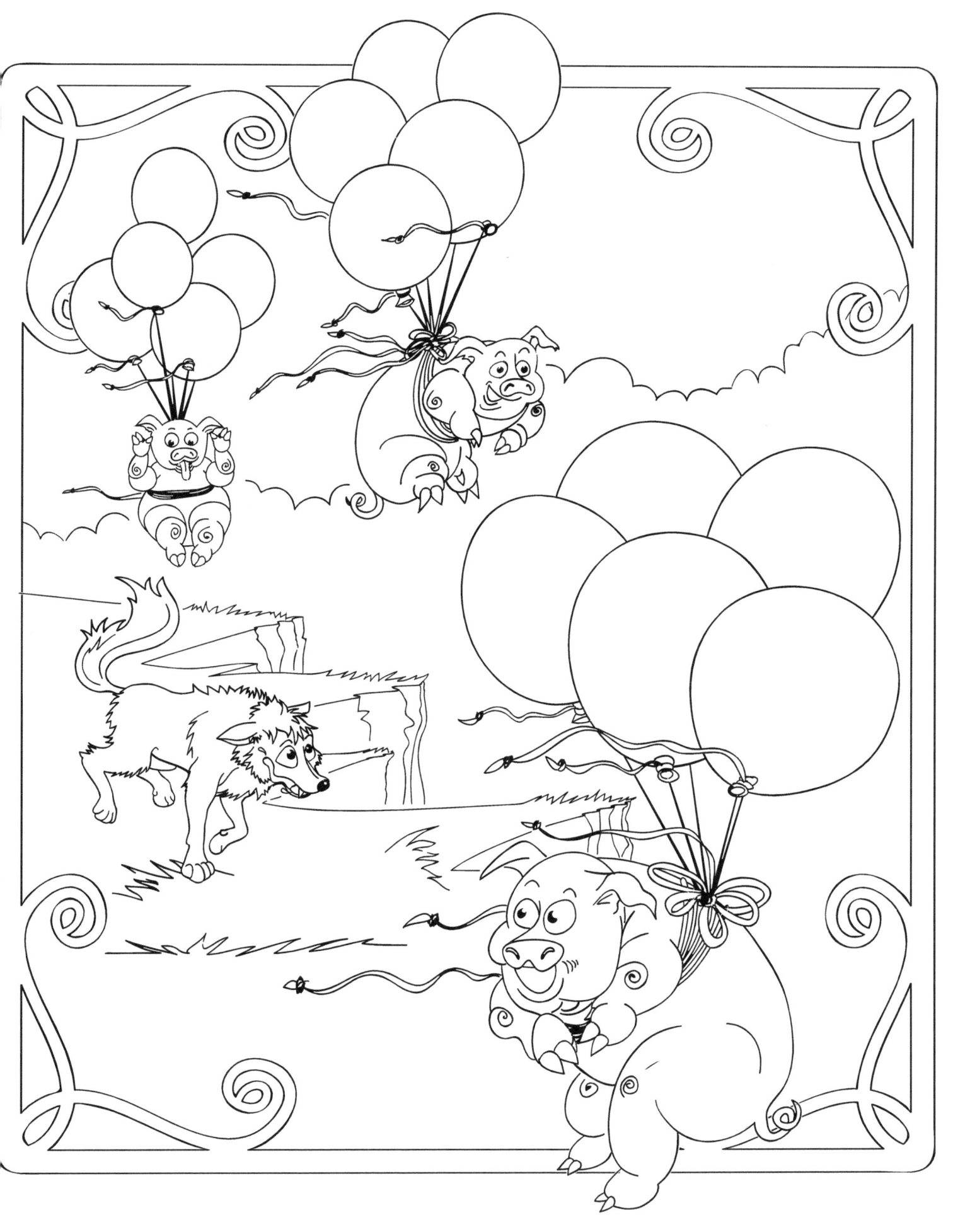

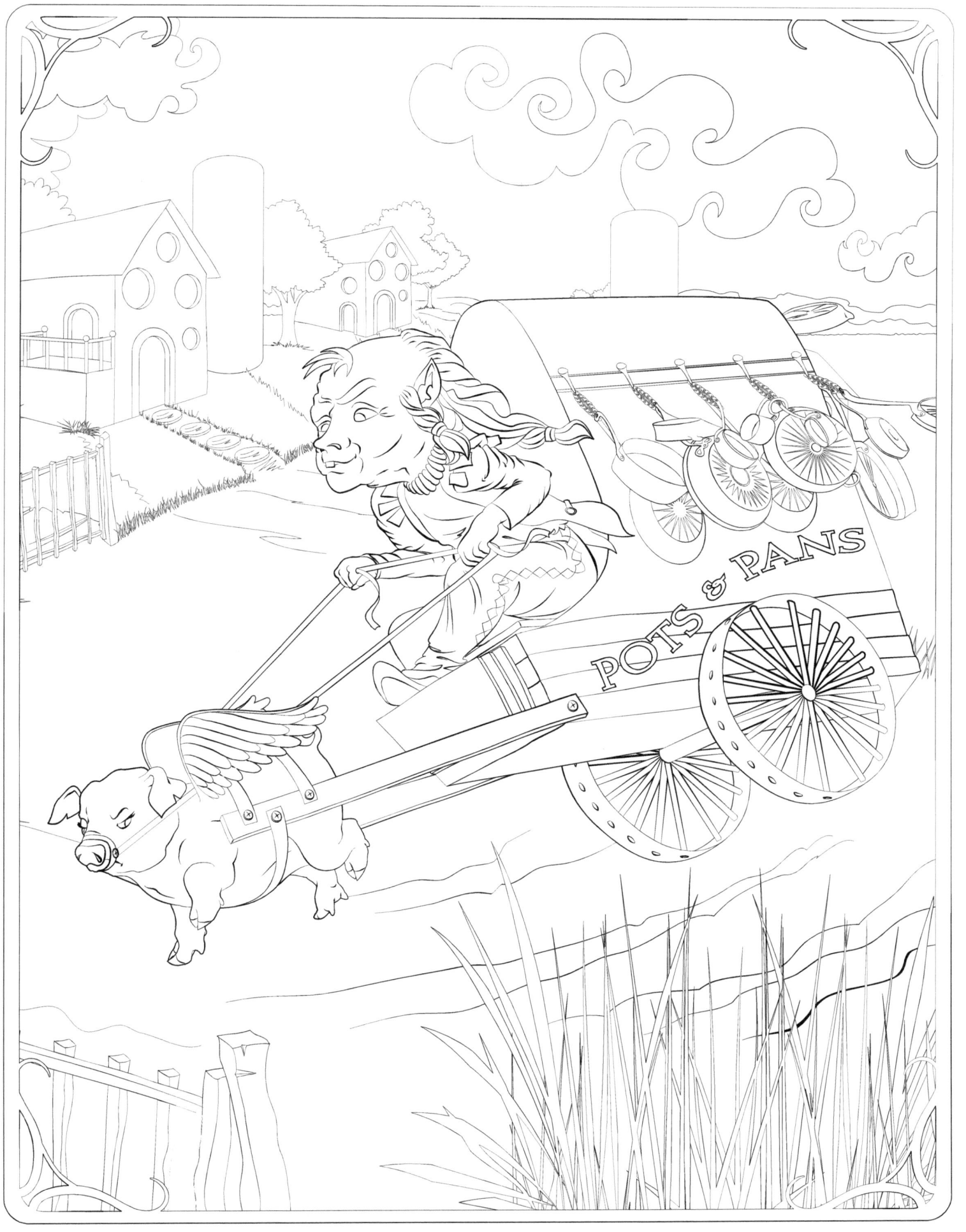

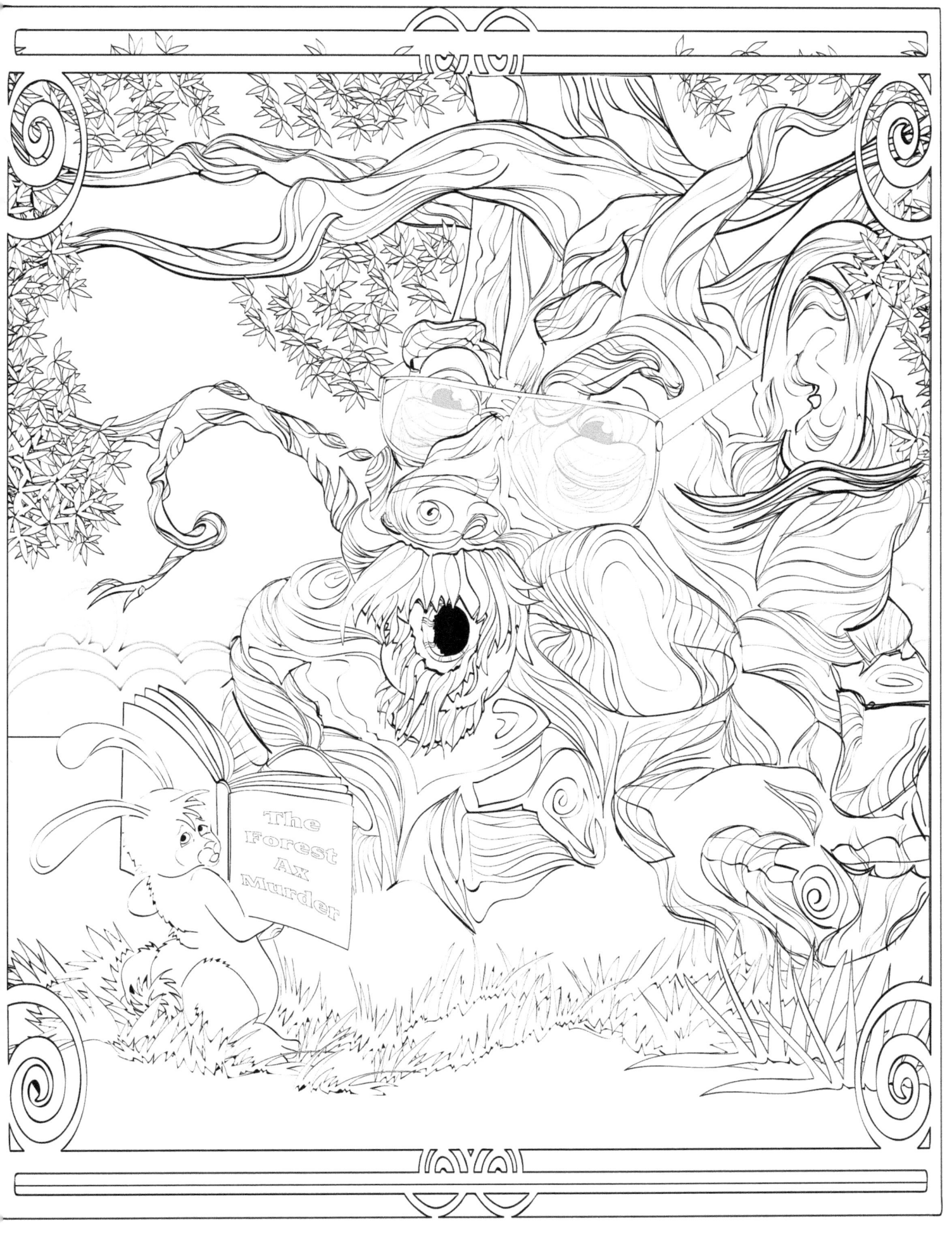

www.ingramcontent.com/pod-product-compliance
Lightning Source LLC
Chambersburg PA
CBHW080613190526
45169CB00007B/2995